Creative Hearts

Works from Two Generations of Poets

Pat Tyrer and Jean Brazelton

Amarillo, Texas

First edition
Copyright © 2017 Pat Tyrer

All rights reserved. This book or portions thereof may not be reproduced in any form without written permission from the publisher or the author except for brief passages used in reviews.

Path Publishing
4302 SW 51st #121
Amarillo, Texas 79109-6159
USA
Path@PathPublishing.com
www.PathPublishing.com

Cover by Path Publishing, CreateSpace, and Pat Tyrer

To order copies, see About Path Publishing at the end of the book.

ISBN-13: 978-1-891774-94-2
ISBN-10: 1-891774-94-8

Printed in the United States of America

DEDICATION

This collection is dedicated to my large, multicultural, multiethnic, and mutigenerational family whom my mother adored and I cherish. Thank you for your love, your dedication to keeping in touch no matter the distance, and your belief in the importance of family ties.

This collection is further dedicated to faith and family as my mother would have wished. How you live is more important than what you believe.

CONTENTS

EXTENDED CONTENTS WITH POEM TITLES	i
PUBLISHER'S NOTE	iii
INTRODUCTION TO THE COLLECTION	v
REMEMBERING	1
GRATITUDE	17
NATURE	29
TRIALS	39
LAUGHTER	49
ACKNOWLEDGEMENTS	54
ABOUT THE AUTHORS	55
ABOUT PATH PUBLISHING	56

EXTENDED CONTENTS WITH POEM TITLES

REMEMBERING 1

When My Life Was Young 2
Penny Poker Dreams 4
One Little Wish 6
Elegy for a Half Sister 8
Lest We Forget 9
Family Ties 10
My Voice Within 11
I Remember You 12
My Quiet Time 14
Remembering Haight Ashbury 15
Villanelle for a Newborn Grandson 16

GRATITUDE 17

Because You Prayed 18
To Aunt Jan on Her 80th Birthday 19
Answered Prayer 20
A Woman Your Age 21
Reach Out! Pray Hard! Hang On! 23
Homage to Poets 24
Sonnet of Myself 25
To Michael on Your 50th Birthday 26
Husband, Father, Friend 28

NATURE 29

Love 30
Western Sun 31
Walking in Palo Duro Canyon in Winter 32
He Cares 34

Harsh Realities 35
Nature Perfect Mother 36
October Trees 37
Morning Moon 38

TRIALS 39

Creation 40
An Only Son 41
Facebook Lies 42
Song for Those Not Yet Dead 43
The Jesus Freak 44
My Church 45
My Plea 46
Wrathful Anger 47
The Call to War 48

LAUGHTER 49

A Psalm of Summer 50
Working Cowboy 51
Cowboy Jack and Jill 52
Killing Gnats 53

PUBLISHER'S NOTE

As a publisher, I have never before requested from my author or poet space in their volume to speak about them to this extent. However, in this case, I have done so. Permission was granted, and I'm thankful.

For years I have admired Dr. Pat Tyrer as a college professor, mother of five, and a lady with a kind and sparkling personality who has generously given her time to educate and encourage local writers beyond her classrooms. When she submitted a query concerning her collection of poems, I was honored. After reading the manuscript, I promptly offered a contract.

It is like her to bring forth the words of her mother, another human being of insight and faith. The woman who gave Pat life is now being given life in the literary world, something she perhaps never seriously considered. Her poems were mostly between her and her God, like in "One Little Wish," where a child wonders what it will be like to live in Heaven.

I praise both of these women for giving us poems about life on all levels, like "An Only Son," where a son is going through a trying time and his mother has to fall back on her spiritual foundations to get her through and to help her son as much as possible, though there is not much she can do. Our children, once they leave home, are like birds on the wing. For Juanita Jean Brazelton, her Patricia Jean has done very well, flying to intellectual and spiritual heights much to be revered.

I'm sure you will enjoy these poems, for they are from the hearts of two women whom I, for one, will never forget.

Pat Tyrer and Jean Brazelton

It is somewhat ironic that just a fortnight before the query was received, I wrote the following poem and dedicated it to Pat. As I explained to her in a cover letter, a few of my 3,000 poems in the last forty years have been about or for other people. Although this poem is not exactly about her life, for I did not know many details, it was sparked by my relationship with her over the last decade.

The Pen and the Crossroads

In my 20's I had a choice: to take a
regular job and write poetry on the side
or teach.
True, by mathematical calculations I can see
I would have written more poems and had
more books published in the former.
But now, after three decades of teaching, I have
a number of what I call "walking poems."
Some of my students are my poems—
they not only speak for me in ways
I never dreamt,
but for the truth in us all.

Dedicated to Dr. Pat Tyrer
John Schmidt

INTRODUCTION TO THE COLLECTION

Several years ago when I was preparing a tribute for my mother for her memorial service, I began searching for the poetry she'd written over the years. After several days looking through boxes, drawers, and trunks, I found only a small selection that she'd saved. Long before the days of computers and printers, these poems were handwritten or typed on an old manual Royal. Yet they were as beautiful and as meaningful as I remembered even as the paper on which they were written had begun to fade. I read her poem, "Love," the day of her memorial as the best representation of the depth of feeling she had written in all of her poetry.

When I decided to put together a collection of my own poetry, I felt that it would be appropriate to combine my work with my mother's. After all, it was she who inspired me to write my own poems. What is presented here is a combined collection of our work. Each poem is identified with [JJB] for Juanita Jean Brazelton or [PJT] for me, Patricia Jean Tyrer at the bottom of each poem. I hope you will enjoy reading these works as much as I enjoyed reviewing, sorting, and collecting them.

Pat Tyrer
Summer 2017

"Mom and me playing cribbage, which was one of our favorite pastimes." Pat

REMEMBERING

Pat Tyrer and Jean Brazelton

WHEN MY LIFE WAS YOUNG

My talks with God are closer now,
Than when my life was young.
I needed Him then when I'd just begun
Just as I do now, that I'm older.
But my cry for His help never left
My lips, and my song was never sung.

I talk to Him now, of
My troubles and woes, and
He's always right there by my side.
I know how He felt of
My days of my youth, and
The tears He must have cried.

His forgiveness of sin of
The life that I led,
When youth was still aglow.
And my future with Him
And His promise He made
Can still and will save my soul.

But my cry is to youth
In these troubled days,
And time passes on so fast.
Don't wait too long, for your
Talk with Him; let Him
Be a part of your past.

Creative Hearts

As life passes by, your life
with Christ, and the beautiful
Memories you'll build
Will not wash away, as
Your troubles soon may. Your
Love for Christ will be fulfilled.

So youth of today, pay heed
To my cry for a better and
brighter tomorrow.
Live your life with Christ
By your side, and there will
Be no time for sorrow. [JJB]

Pat Tyrer and Jean Brazelton

PENNY POKER DREAMS

I awoke last night in the grip of memory,
    voices yelling, "Ma, are you playing?"
Slippers shuffling across wooden floors the only answer.
Poker pennies in coffee cans, "Ante up, Ruthie, in or out"
    assaults my ears with gravely brusqueness.

Lying on the living room floor too few feet away,
    Pinkie nips at my ankles between incessant barking as
    Petey Bird scatters seeds here and there,
    his repetitious "pretty boy" his only redemption.

I am young; I dream of the boy across the street,
    and Elvis asks if I am lonesome
    while around me rustles the soft flow of cotton dusters,
    covered snaps and pockets full of hankies smelling of
    Mentholatum.

I raise my head, surprised to hear, "Walt, come on,"
    to one I only know as Uncle Bud.
Sleek black panther with red glass eyes watches me from atop
    the Philco.
Mary and Nita stare down from graduation smiles.

"Charlie, Ma, are you in or out?"
    reverberates from the dining room poker table.
Strong hands deal cards, read by the same eyes
    peering out from different faces.

Memory moves to a different time and everyone comes.
Uncle Carl at the door, whispered tears, "Billy's gone."
Young cousins, noisy and irreverent, terrorize Great Uncle
    Bill with giggles uncontained by youthful hands.

Creative Hearts

Aunt Dodo "sh's" as Aunt Bea scolds, "behave."
We melt into muffled giggles, tripping over each other,
    Aunt Eleanor's grin our only ally.
Sadness we sense but don't understand;
    sadness mitigated by plates of potato salad and Aunt
    Evelyn's apple pie.

Summer evenings catching lightning bugs,
    antsy to go home, mom and Aunt Bea at the kitchen
    table.
Cigarettes and coffee, companionship I don't understand,
"Why don't you kids go see Uncle Bud?" we're told.

I am young and time lasts forever. "Talk later, Mom."
I whine, pulling on the edge of her white uniform,
    looking up into twin faces, indifferent to my youthful
    misery.
Loving smiles suffer my indifference.

Goodbye hugs and kisses from lips which smell of coffee and
    cigarettes.
Michael, sleepy on the porch, curled against the wicker chair.
"See you later," I holler from the departing car window.
And turn away from the house on Jones Street. [PJT]

Pat Tyrer and Jean Brazelton

ONE LITTLE WISH

If I could have one wish come
true to be with God forever.
And from His strong and faithful
hand I would not ever wander.

But I am just a little child
And I must wait for signs
That God will give, when He wants
And thinks that it's my time.

To go beyond the farthest land
And from the deepest sea
Where God and Twelve Disciples
Will be waiting there for me.

A golden harp they'll give to me,
And with God's angels I'll sing,
And walk in the Heavenly valley
Where peace is so serene.

Where men and women free
From care, and happiness is found.
Where little children have a place
on this eternal ground.

But I am just a little child
And I must wait for that sign
That God will give to me, He said,
When He thinks it's my time.

So go beyond that farthest land
And from the deepest sea
Where Jesus, Joseph, and Mary be,
They're there to welcome me. [JJB]

Pat Tyrer and Jean Brazelton

ELEGY FOR A HALF SISTER

When Paula died the air was still
against my cheek. The willow wept in ordinary measure,
rain clouds and dusty earth yet unaffected
poet's claim in sad laments unheard and undigested.

Photographs to seize upon to spare the souls of
those of us with nonexistent memories.
Recollections thin with grief of possibilities,
yearly cards define too thin a relationship.

"My sister died today," cannot be said with clear integrity
for she an unknown entity; more genetic than familial.
No resurrected sympathy of empty knowledge
to be digested alone in somber contemplation. [PJT]

LEST WE FORGET

They cry their need for love so loud.
They demonstrate for mankind proud.
But yet, a lonely cry we hear
Could it be just a cry of fear?

They do need love, but don't we all
When chips are down, we tend to fall.
To rant and rave, like youth today
When trouble seems to find our way.

The cries and troubles could be small
If only we'd learn before we fall.
He's ready to help, but what do we say
It's been so long, I forgot how to pray. [JJB]

Pat Tyrer and Jean Brazelton

FAMILY TIES

Secrets hidden in DNA.
Results don't coincide.
Oft-told tales must all make way
For genes which do not lie.

Results don't coincide
With legends told of England's best
For genes which do not lie.
Show none from there came here to rest.

With legends told of England's best
Among the gravestones planted deep
Show none from there came here to rest.
Whose bones these are that herein sleep.

Among the gravestones planted deep
Beneath familiar family name.
Whose bones these are that herein sleep.
Perhaps a less-than famous claim.

Beneath familiar family name.
Oft-told tales must all make way
Perhaps a less-than famous claim.
Secrets hidden in DNA. [PJT]

MY VOICE WITHIN

When the quiet voice
Within me speaks
To calm my weary soul,

God grant me grace of
Stillness until it's message
I've been told.

Let not my own proud selfish
Thought try to change
The words.

God grant me grace to
Understand, the message
That I've heard. [JJB]

Pat Tyrer and Jean Brazelton

I REMEMBER YOU

I remember you; one shoulder leaning
against the door frame. Kitchen light
casting a halo against your curly black hair,
long, unkempt. Your blue eyes, bright, glistening.

You're on my mind today, here and now.
Keeping company on the porch swing
as I drink my tea and watch the rain
dribble down the screen door.

Your presence is heavy
like the lag edging the porch,
the slatted floorboards wet
from the weight of weather.

There's no lightness to your being
long passed into the grave
no ethereal form fancifully
filling the room.

You are a weight,
a heavy tome descended
on my shoulders. Your essence,
a soul-deadening weight.

Today of all days I remember you.
The pressure of your love
the rain and low fog
Jefferson Airplane on the radio.

I remember when we were.
The future full. Do you recall
before the pain, the ache of
all we lost as we gained.

Unprepared, we were, for the rain,
the cold; the wicked winds of failure
too quickly fading light,
mountains of dark emotion.

So busy surviving, our dream rained
out. We didn't notice our goals
lost under piles of emotional
snow too deep to be uncovered.

Our youthful dreams washed away.
Destroyed by torrents of loss,
love torn from our arms
like the detritus of a raging flood.

The memory of your blue eyes
survive the memories of our failure.
Your smile and laughter
just fading moments of lost time. [PJT]

Pat Tyrer and Jean Brazelton

MY QUIET TIME

One hour a day I rest my mind from the daily cares around.
And let my thoughts go back in time where happiness is
 found.
Sometimes I wonder back in time where childhood was gay,
 to the old white house on the corner lot where I used to
 run and play.
I see my friends of yesteryear with faces all aglow
 and listen as they call my name, on the old familiar road.
These memories are so fresh and real for me to keep and
 share
With anyone who passes by who has no one to care. [JJB]

REMEMBERING HAIGHT ASHBURY

I dream of a yellow Volkswagen covered in psychedelic
 flowers
stuck at the top of Haight Street, the boot tied with
 clothesline,
slipping a few inches with each grinding of the gears
when at last, engine roaring, it tops the crest and is gone.

The years are reflected in the store window
still selling pipes and paraphernalia and papers
for we who cling to the past and long for understanding
of what we accomplished with anger and flags on our jeans.

Tell me about the sixties they whine with curiosity to hear
of drugs and debauchery unknown to them by disease and
 distilled
history of meaningful encounters and brave wooden soldiers
fighting and dying and flowers remembered in aging stories.

Summers of love a cliché so strong it barely survives
 remembering
when possibility felt real and hope gathered energy and action
before Charlie and murder and mayhem and Manson
shattered forever the possibility of innocence and music and
 maybe. [PJT]

Pat Tyrer and Jean Brazelton

VILLANELLE FOR A NEWBORN GRANDSON

Fresh and new at two days old.
Smiling at my furrowed face.
Alert and set for life to unfold.

Your voyage to start, your path untold.
The hours go fast like precious gold.
Fresh and new at two days old.

Still hesitant, you're not yet bold.
But worry not, it's quite the race.
Alert and set for life to unfold.

The years will move along tenfold.
Days will pass without a trace.
Fresh and new at two days old.

Enjoy the journey you'll behold.
Remember life is filled with grace.
Alert and set for life to unfold.

Today you're young, your life untold.
Today is gone with bare a trace.
Fresh and new at two days old
Alert and set for life to unfold. [PJT]

GRATITUDE

Pat Tyrer and Jean Brazelton

BECAUSE YOU PRAYED

Because you prayed for me,
I found the strength I needed for my task.
The courage I had lacked before
The faith to see beyond my narrow world;
New joy for pain I found, and the zeal
To press on forward strong of heart again
    Because you prayed.

Because you prayed for me,
I found it was not hard to face the dawn,
Take up the work I laid away but yesterday
And do it, and dare to smile a
Bit, and found a blessing I'd not
Dreamed was there.
    Because you prayed.

Because you prayed for me,
Tonight, I seem to reach and find
Your hand close by as I had known
It would be. It was as though
God, to our hearts, had softly whispered "peace."
    Because you prayed. [JJB]

TO AUNT JAN ON HER 80TH BIRTHDAY

A life so full; eight decades long.
Gracious, loving, giving, strong.
Surrounded now by generations
thankful for your ministrations.

A legacy of kind compassion,
eighty years of benefaction.
Time to rest? Oh no, not yet.
In the future comes the best.

Light our lives for years to come.
Teach us how to overcome.
Share your wisdom with us all
till your Savior comes to call.

We've much to learn and you've the key
to lead us to eternity.
With lots of time on bended knee
you've lived a life of which He's pleased. [PJT]

Pat Tyrer and Jean Brazelton

ANSWERED PRAYER

I've walked and run on
This God-given land.

In search of another
With an outstretched hand.

Like an answered prayer
You came my way.

With your outstretched hand
Full of love that day. [JJB]

A WOMAN YOUR AGE

"For a woman your age" I'm told and retold
"You're astonishingly fine," as if fine were
a special code indicating pleasantly
fit, incredibly fetching, or possessing finesse.

"For a woman your age" a familiar refrain,
"Life is full and complete." Familiar words that really
mean old, but not gone quite gone. Am I dying
or dead, I wonder now that I'm a woman my age?

"For a woman my age," I'm surprisingly pleased
with myself. My intentions are known;
my habits are set; I'm finally all grown, and
I have no regrets for "a woman my age." [PJT]

Pat Tyrer and Jean Brazelton

REACH OUT! PRAY HARD! HANG ON!

There's a bit of good philosophy
That I'd like to pass along,
Just in case of gloomy weather
Or you lack a smile or song.
Or an ache or pain is troubling
Or just everything goes wrong.
Just remember this one message:
Reach out! Pray hard! Hang on!

When your faith in someone tumbles
And you know you've been misled,
When the cynic and the critic
Try to tell you God is dead,
When your hopes and dreams have faded
And it seems they're almost gone,
Then is the time you need this message:
Reach out! Pray hard! Hang on!

Oh, it won't remove the shadows
But they'll seem to lift awhile,
And your friends may not have changed much
But you can face them with a smile.
And the mountain that seemed destined
To block your way has gone
If you'll follow this one signpost:
Reach out! Pray hard! Hang on!

Creative Hearts

I won't guarantee you'll prosper
Far beyond your wildest dreams,
Or that all your circumstances
Will be better than they seem;
But I will surely promise
Better pathways farther on.
Trust in our Heavenly Father:
Reach out! Pray hard! Hang on! [JJB]

Pat Tyrer and Jean Brazelton

HOMAGE TO POETS

They say that those who can't, will teach, for lack
of skills to write, or reach an audience
composed of peers. I cannot make a rhyme
or poem that's fit to print upon a sign
for marketing or just to read in spring
when love is freshly green and grown like grass.

So what else can I do but teach—explore
the modes, the forms, the lines of ever growing
little minds which as the metaphor of sponge
so captures all they've done or yet to do.
And yet I want to spread my wings and sing
about the lovely things that poets write.

I form the words and find the tropes that make
the images conform to what I feel
is true and natural. Yet still they lie
upon the page like fallen leaves in great
disgrace for once they lived in others' hands
where shades of colored meaning gave them life.

Upon the Muses, I depend for every
single word I write. I take no credit
for the gifts that Fortune gives with great
delight. The words which flow upon the page
show wisdom far beyond the grace of such
a poet as myself could offer here without their help. [PJT]

SONNET OF MYSELF

I am a poem of fourteen lines of verse
who needs to have a rhythm to my life.
I prattle forth and sometimes may seem terse.
To me my sense of order seems just fine.

Precise and balanced well from stem to stern
I sail along with confidence and glee.
I know just where I'm going at each turn
and grateful, balanced, happy to be me.

I know a life of structure's not for some.
What kind of world would that be after all,
with every single person being one
like dancers all in rhythm at a ball.

However, just for me the rules are fine.
No matter if I do live out of time. [PJT]

Pat Tyrer and Jean Brazelton

TO MICHAEL ON YOUR 50TH BIRTHDAY

I REMEMBER when you were shorter than me.
I remember teaching you how to make chicken noodle soup when we walked home from Hunt Elementary School at lunch time.
I remember celebrating New Year's Eve 1959 with miniature sandwiches and a bottle of root beer.
I remember making butter cookies on a Sunday afternoon.
I remember your watching Johnny Carson and eating a platter full of Chef Boyardee spaghetti.
I remember taking a taped tour of your house in Florida.
I remember watching you hold your son.
I remember your tears of joy at my son's wedding.
I remember the look on your face and the light in your eyes when you introduced me to Pam.
I remember your delight eating cotton candy at the circus.
I remember the hug you gave me when you were in the hospital.
I remember the joy in your voice when you told me about your new job.

I SHOULD HAVE TOLD YOU how much I adored you when you were little.
I should have told you that making chicken soup was easy.
I should have told you that New Year's Eve 1959 was one of my happiest.
I should have let you help make butter cookies.
I should have known Johnny Carson wasn't THAT funny!
I should have written you more when you were in the Navy.
I should have spent more time with you and your family.
I should have thanked you for coming to California.
I should have told you how delighted I was that you found Pam.
I should have told you how scared I was when you were in the hospital.

I should have told you how proud I was that you'd become so successful.

I WANT YOU TO KNOW that I've always loved you and always will.
I want you to know how proud I am of your accomplishments.
I want you to know what a great father and a loving husband I think you are.
I want you to know how much I brag about you to my friends.
I want you to know how intelligent and clever I think you are.
I want you to know how much I think about you every day.
I want you to know how funny and entertaining I think you are.
I want you to know how glad I am that you're my brother and my friend.
I want you to know how sorry I am that I'm not there with you today. [PJT]

Pat Tyrer and Jean Brazelton

HUSBAND, FATHER, FRIEND

Some see your competence; I see your patience
Tailored to accept what becomes you with grace.
Ever faithful and just, you reflect an inner strength
Very few can maintain with understanding and
Equanimity granted to so few.

Tender and loving as father and friend,
You've given the best that you could
Regardless of what life placed in your path.
Endurance and gratitude your life words.
Rejoined with thankfulness, refinement, and love. [PJT]

NATURE

Pat Tyrer and Jean Brazelton

LOVE

"Help me Father to give thanks
for the gentle rain, sunny skies,

For home and friends,
but most of all, for love."

Some people say it's hard to find
A love that you can share.

A love that doesn't require more
Than just a sign you care.

A touch of a hand, a word when needed
Is all it should require.

To grow so large and encompass all
Who have the same desire.

To find this love you only need
Another soul nearby.

Who wants this love, the same as you
But only afraid to try.

Reach out and touch this human hand
And see what it can do.

The warmth of love will fill your soul
This warmth, He'll share with you. [JJB]

WESTERN SUN

The sun slips off the western sky,
its reddened breath floating high
and leaving dusk alone to bid
goodnight to shadows barely dim.

And early in the summer morn,
it then returns in brighter form
beginning pale, it rises high
coloring red it crosses by.

Midday burning hot and bright,
high against the coming night
till early eve arrives unbidden
to make us long for night still hidden. [PJT]

Pat Tyrer and Jean Brazelton

WALKING IN PALO DURO CANYON IN WINTER

I like walking where the wind is rarely quiet
and the evening star glows brightly,
a consistent presence lying over the canyon
pushing the sun along, urging the moon
to follow its intense track like the creek now dusty
and disregarded until spring's outburst of life.

Winter on the high plains is not an easy life
for anyone or thing or being driven mad by the quiet
whip of the wind as it crosses the plains flat and dusty,
where only the aged mesquite blooming brightly
signals the end of winter, and the orbit of the spring moon
lights the crevices where the vulnerable hide in the canyon.

It's fascinating to watch the snow fall in the canyon,
covering flora and fauna alike with no regard of life
on varying scales of existence beneath the winter moon
crouching, hidden in crevices, waiting for the quiet
dampening the snow brings, where shadows brightly
dance against the landscape once dry and dusty.

I walk where the snow and the ground, still dusty,
wait for the drifts to descend the walls of the canyon.
Where the sun has long given way to sky brightly
lit by earth's companion, a slumbering bath of life
flooding the floor of the canyon, hushed and quiet
like the foot of Neil Armstrong as it touched the moon.

In the crevice where the light from the full moon
has yet to reach the smallest of bobcats lying in his dusty
den, only his golden ocher eyes revealing his quiet
watch for an unsuspecting victim crossing the canyon.
In the depths of winter when the snow falls, life
is hidden or beneath ground, slumbering, dreaming brightly

of warmer days and gentler nights where desires brightly
formed fill the arroyo with the sweetness of a summer moon
and aoudad sheep and diamondbacks hunt lesser life,
themselves living on such as is hidden in the dusty
fissures of the Spanish Skirts high up walls of the canyon,
their gray, yellow and lavender stone swishing in the quiet.

Imaginary dancers prance beneath a brightly shining moon,
their footsteps awaking the sleeping life from their dusty beds
and echoing the voices of long ago, now quiet, in the canyon.
[PJT]

Pat Tyrer and Jean Brazelton

HE CARES

I know that I can trust the Lord
To keep the stars in place,
To grant the lark, the rose, the oak,
His wisdom and His grace.

I know that I can trust the Lord
To send the morning light,
To turn each winter into spring,
To rule each depth, each height. [JJB]

HARSH REALITIES

I read the West from atop the bluff
hanging over unseen life too small to notice
and of no use to even the coyotes.

Ragged brush nearly covers the paths
between the rocks, righteous in its authority
to squeeze out the slighter undergrowth.

Mesquite quietly waits for the un-initiated
vulnerable to its razor-like spurs
ready to entangle the unwary.

Ragged skies bring sudden bursts
which swallow lesser creatures
foolishly sunning in the dusty burn. [PJT]

Pat Tyrer and Jean Brazelton

NATURE PERFECT MOTHER

Nature is a perfect mother who knows when
a fluttering leaf becomes disconnected from life,
it's withered edges nothing more than shriveling veins
as the odor of death drizzles down its stem.

A lost child, addicted and rootless
living on poison drizzling into his veins.
Sleeping in a car twenty feet from my door, yet
rejecting my pleas to intercede in his dying.

My ranting and pleading and crying does
little to change the path upon which he travels,
ever spiraling closer to death. His path dark
and loathsome, yet I cannot turn away.

Nature speaks softly like a mother cooing to her child,
an ancient caretaker filled with patience.
She's pragmatic, and unlike me,
able to cut away that which cannot thrive. [PJT]

OCTOBER TREES

Quietly returning to their peaceful slumber,
the maples murmur words of grace, as
the red oaks whisper a patch of melody.

Winds echoing breezes softly cooing
to the forest—an ancient caretaker.
Patient, pragmatic and enduring.

Fluttering leaves finished with life.
Withered edges shriveled and crackling
blanket of yellow, red, and gold.

Matted on the forest floor sustaining
nature's sleeping presence,
through winter's frigid spell. [PJT]

MORNING MOON

Morning moon still bright, accomplice
to morning coffee on the screened porch.
Seat still damp with dew and blighted by age,
but rocking with the grain of the wood.

Nature's melody still a solo act.
Only the smallest of the birds
highest in the trees hear the sun
chasing the moon away. [PJT]

TRIALS

Pat Tyrer and Jean Brazelton

CREATION

Oh God of all creation
How can You be so still,
While men of many nations
Harm, destroy, and kill.

Oh God of all creation
How can You be so still
While little children suffer
The pain of hunger so real.

Oh God of all creation
How can You be so still
When our brothers' cry for freedom
Still rings from distant hills.

Oh God of all creation
Most merciful Father to all
We seek forgiveness, Father,
For not hearing our brothers' call.

Oh God, forgive our stillness.
We've heard Your message clear.
Your voice was firm but gentle,
Your love was felt so near.

Oh God of all creation
Teach us what to pray
So we may help our fellowman
To seek Your help today. [JJB]

AN ONLY SON

I try not to think of you in jail
sitting behind bars
locked up, separated from
the world you know.

I try not to think about what
you've done and
whether it reflects upon
me as your mother.

I try not to think about whether
you've changed for the better,
because that's how you
sound on the telephone.

I try not to think about
your future and
what will happen to you
after I'm gone. [PJT]

FACEBOOK LIES

The photos on Facebook
filled with smiling faces
of birthdays and holidays
lurks an underlying current of
grief and resentment
of drug addition and alcoholism,
the aftermath of angry voices
failed negotiations, memories
edged in hostilities never
confronted.

If the photos were
in colors of emotion, the
aftermath of extinguished
candles, the detritus of holiday
gatherings, they'd be photos
not even the hardiest
among us could endure
to stare at, searching the
faces of families who
never were family. [PJT]

SONG FOR THOSE NOT YET DEAD

A song about the sinful dead
  For those who've sailed beyond the sea
Their flesh decays and yet they cry
        out for their deeds.

And now they suffer life's regrets
  Ashamed of those they cannot change.
They cry to God, "forgive my debts,"
        But it's too late.

Pretend that you're among the dead
  Without a hope to save your soul.
The path that lies before you now
        Is one you can control.

Beware of time that flies away
  Ahead there lies the empty grave.
Your soul's your own, of that you're right,
        but also yours to save. [PJT]

Pat Tyrer and Jean Brazelton

THE JESUS FREAK

I met a young man the other day
They call him a Jesus freak.
His hair was long; his face unshaved,
His clothes were far from neat.

I listened as he told his tale
How drugs had been his game.
And how he found this Jesus, man,
His style of life did change.

I looked upon this youthful face
And saw a light shine through.
There was no doubt the light I saw
Was from the Jesus that I knew too. [JJB]

MY CHURCH

My church is an impressive place,
Stained windows, carpet, and all.

But I wonder how my Lord would feel
If He were to come make a call.

Would He be impressed by the money
That's spent on this place we call His house?

Or would the tears run from His eyes
For the needy who are going without? [JJB]

Pat Tyrer and Jean Brazelton

MY PLEA

My God, My God
Can You hear my plea?
Have I asked too much?
Have You turned on me?

Are You not my shepherd
Who will guide my way
Through dark of night,
Through light of day?

I know that You love me.
I know that You care.
By compassion You show me
With each grief that I bear.

My plea may be selfish,
Forgiveness I seek,
So my soul will not perish
And Your love I may keep. [JJB]

WRATHFUL ANGER

red and glaring hot
miasma venting stream
flowing off the flames
of darkened broken dreams

spouting cask of fire
grizzled molten lake
ever burning pyre of
scalding pungent ache

never to be cooled
by love's unrivaled will
deep within the fire dwelling
never to be stilled [PJT]

Pat Tyrer and Jean Brazelton

THE CALL TO WAR

I loved a boy who loved me more
Than he could best express,
So he went to war to answer for
What he could do the best.

We fell in love so long before
When he was whole as me,
But now he's back, he's even more
Morose than he used to be.

Our lives have changed; adjustments made
Our sympathies run out
The memories of war won't fade
The helplessness and doubt.

The patriotic bands are done
The flags all put aside
Hailed as heroes, mothers' sons
At least we know they tried.

But images of wars persist
The papers speak of death
Calls for heroes once again,
Enlist! Enlist! Enlist!

It matters not how many die,
Nor how we count the toll
The young will hear the battle cry
Prepared to give their all. [PJT]

LAUGHTER

Pat Tyrer and Jean Brazelton

A PSALM OF SUMMER

Now it came to pass that spring turned
To summer again.

God's people raised
Their voices and said:

Recreation is my shepherd,
I shall not stay at home.

He maketh me to lie down in a
Sleeping bag.

He restoreth my suntan.

He leadeth me to state parks
For comfort's sake.

Even though I stray on the Lord's day,
I will fear no reprimand.

Thou art with me. My rod and my
Reel, they comfort me.

I anoitest my skin with oil,
My gas tank runneth over.

Surely my trailer will follow me
All the weekends this summer.

I shall return to the Lord's house this fall.

But then it is hunting season
And that's another Psalm. [JJB]

WORKING COWBOY

His spurs click and jangle as he walks the aisle of the
　　supermarket
unaware of the titters of the schoolgirl cashiers.

The starched crease of his jeans ends at frayed cuffs
resting atop boots worn and softened by the harsh Texas
　　wind.

The not unpleasant smell of grit and leather
fills the air around his swagger.

Selections bagged, head cocked, bruised forefinger rises to tap
　　the brim
of his Stetson as he strolls out into the parking lot. [PJT]

Pat Tyrer and Jean Brazelton

COWBOY JACK AND JILL

Cowboy Jack and his gal Jill
drove their cattle up the hill
up the mountain steep and high
cool fresh water was their guide.

Cattle know the way to go;
they often travel to and fro'
winter, summer, spring, and fall,
the weathered path has seen it all.

Jack and Jill, they spend their time
keeping count along the line
'til the weather starts to chill, then
time to drive them down the hill. [PJT]

KILLING GNATS

I'm killing gnats with my hands because
they're small and my hands are big and
there's a bit of ego involved; besides,
they're mildly annoying and the act
of smashing them and wiping away the black
dot of their existence is immorally satisfying. [PJT]

ACKNOWLEDGEMENTS

"Harsh Realities," previously published by *Plum Tree Tavern*, 2016

"Penny Poker Dreams," a version of this piece was previously published by *The Houston Literary Review*, 2008

"Remembering Haight Ashbury," performed for *National Council of Teachers of English*, National Poetry Month, 2006

"Sonnet of Myself," previously published by *Forms Quarterly*, 2015

"Walking in Palo Duro Canyon in Winter," previously published by *The Penwood Review*, 2015

"Working Cowboy," previously published by *The Houston Literary Review*, 2008

ABOUT THE AUTHORS

Juanita Jean (Hoaas) Brazelton was born in Dakota City, Nebraska in 1929 and for most of her adult life lived in Sioux City, Iowa and Ankeny, Iowa. She was a doctor's nurse by trade. Her faith, her family, and her church were of utmost importance to her and are the subjects of her poetry. Jean, as she preferred to be called, joined our Lord in the summer of 2008.

Patricia Jean (Brazelton) Tyrer is a Professor of English at West Texas A&M University in Canyon, Texas where she lives with her husband and two dogs. Pat teaches creative writing and American literature. She enjoys bird watching in Palo Duro Canyon during the day and star gazing at night. She can be reached at tyrer@suddenlink.net or through her website at www.wtamu.edu/~ptyrer.

Pat Tyrer and Jean Brazelton

ABOUT PATH PUBLISHING

Path Publishing began in 1993 and has published a variety of uplifting books and other projects over the years. We tend to specialize in general and Christian nonfiction, poetry, biographies, and self-help. Our website, PathPublishing.com, contains the works of many writers. In the past we have been listed in these publications: *Christian Writers' Market Guide*, *The Directory of Little Magazines and Small Presses*, and *The Writer*.

To order a paperback copy of *Creative Hearts: Works from Two Generations of Poets*, purchase at Amazon.com or use the PayPal shopping cart at PathPublishing.com. You can also send $11.99 plus $3.50 shipping for a total of $15.49 (Texans add 8.25 percent sales tax for a total of $16.77) to Path Publishing, 4302 SW 51st #121, Amarillo, Texas 79109-6159.

www.ingramcontent.com/pod-product-compliance
Lightning Source LLC
Chambersburg PA
CBHW071637040426
42452CB00009B/1661